MOVE AND GET HEALTHY!

MAKE A MEAL PLAN: SMART FOOD SHOPPING

WRITTEN BY
SUSAN TEMPLE KESSELRING

ILLUSTRATED BY
TATEVIK AVAKYAN

FRESH APPLES!

magic wagon

Content Consultant:
Pamela Van Zyl York,
MPH, PhD, RD, LN

VISIT US AT WWW.ABDOPUBLISHING.COM

Published by Magic Wagon, a division of the ABDO Group, PO Box 398166, Minneapolis, MN 55439. Copyright © 2012 by Abdo Consulting Group, Inc. International copyrights reserved in all countries. All rights reserved. No part of this book may be reproduced in any form without written permission from the publisher.

Looking Glass Library™ is a trademark and logo of Magic Wagon.

Printed in the United States of America, North Mankato, Minnesota.
102011
012012
 THIS BOOK CONTAINS AT LEAST 10% RECYCLED MATERIALS.

Text by Susan Temple Kesselring
Illustrations by Tatevik Avakyan
Edited by Melissa York
Series design and cover production by Emily Love
Interior production by Craig Hinton

Library of Congress Cataloging-in-Publication Data

Kesselring, Susan.
  Make a meal plan : smart food shopping / by Susan Temple Kesselring ; illustrated by Tatevik Avakyan.
      p. cm. -- (Move and get healthy!)
  Includes index.
  ISBN 978-1-61641-863-2
  1. Grocery shopping--Juvenile literature. 2. Diet therapy for children--Juvenile literature. 3. Children--Nutrition--Juvenile literature. I. Title.
  TX356.K47 2012
  640.73--dc23
                            2011033085

TABLE OF CONTENTS

HEALTHFUL FOOD FOR A HEALTHY BODY

Food is fuel for your body. Eating healthful food gives you energy. It tastes good. Healthful foods have lots of nutrients. Nutrients keep you healthy. They help you grow.

You can help your family plan healthful meals and shop for healthful food. You can also help prepare the foods you eat.

MILK

SKIM

5

Dairy Foods

Vegetables

Foods with Protein

Fruits

Foods Made from Grain

6

You need to eat many different types of food. Divide your plate in half at every meal. Half your plate should be fruits and vegetables. The other half should be foods with protein and foods made from grains. Eat dairy foods at every meal, too. By doing this, you will follow the government's suggested meal plan called MyPlate.

TYPES OF FOOD

There are five basic food groups. They are:

fruits: apples, pears, bananas, berries

vegetables: broccoli, spinach, celery, carrots

foods with protein: meat, fish, eggs, black or baked beans

dairy foods: milk, yogurt, cheese

foods made from grains: bread, rice, cereal, pasta. Look for whole wheat and whole grain foods. Whole grain foods are full of nutrients!

PLAN HEALTHFUL MEALS

Eating and cooking at home is tasty and fun. When you cook, you choose the ingredients. You know exactly what you are eating.

Make a plan with your family before you go food shopping. Talk about the next few days. Look at recipes. Write down each day and each meal. Plan to eat different types of food at each meal.

Now, look to see what ingredients you need. A grown-up should check what food you already have at home. Make a list of items you need to buy.

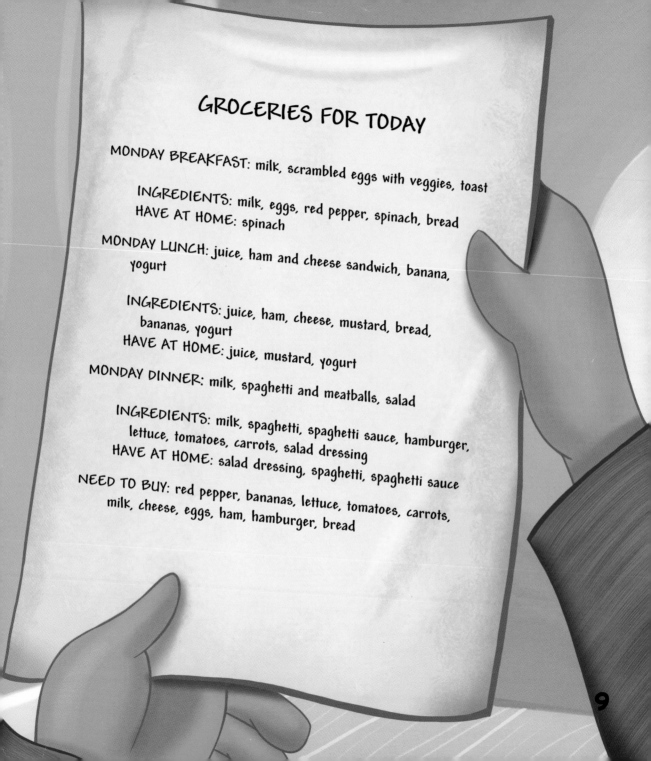

GROCERIES FOR TODAY

MONDAY BREAKFAST: milk, scrambled eggs with veggies, toast

    INGREDIENTS: milk, eggs, red pepper, spinach, bread
    HAVE AT HOME: spinach

MONDAY LUNCH: juice, ham and cheese sandwich, banana, yogurt

    INGREDIENTS: juice, ham, cheese, mustard, bread, bananas, yogurt
    HAVE AT HOME: juice, mustard, yogurt

MONDAY DINNER: milk, spaghetti and meatballs, salad

    INGREDIENTS: milk, spaghetti, spaghetti sauce, hamburger, lettuce, tomatoes, carrots, salad dressing
    HAVE AT HOME: salad dressing, spaghetti, spaghetti sauce

NEED TO BUY: red pepper, bananas, lettuce, tomatoes, carrots, milk, cheese, eggs, ham, hamburger, bread

FOOD ALLERGIES

Some people are allergic to foods, such as nuts, chocolate, and even certain fruits and vegetables. If you are having snacks with friends, be sure to find out if they have allergies first so you can make a snack plan!

SNACKS AND SWEETS

Plan for snacks and sweets. Eat a healthful snack when you are hungry between meals. A healthful snack gives you energy. You need energy to play and learn.

Have a small sweet after one meal a day. Try fruits such as melons, strawberries, grapes, or pears instead of cookies or candy.

SOME HEALTHFUL SNACKS

Yogurt

Nuts such as peanuts, cashews, or almonds

Peanut butter on apples or celery

Carrot sticks

Cheese sticks

Dried fruit

Whole-grain crackers

WHAT TO EXPECT AT THE STORE

Many grocery stores look similar. Ask for a map of the store. Most stores put signs above each aisle. The signs tell what food is there. Or ask a grocery store worker for help.

Dairy foods, meats, and fruits and vegetables are often along the walls. These foods are kept in cold cases. Some stores have a bakery or a meat counter.

The middle of the store has many aisles. The aisles have boxed food, canned food, frozen foods, dried foods, and foods that do not go in the refrigerator.

SHOPPING TIP

Similar foods are usually close together in the store. On your shopping list, put the vegetables and fruits together. Put the dairy foods together. This will save time at the store.

Meats

 Dairy

 Canned Foods

 Frozen Foods

 Grains & Cereal

 Produce

Registers

13

FRESH, FROZEN, DRIED, OR CANNED?

Many foods come in several different forms. You can buy fresh green beans. Fresh beans are whole and not cooked. You can buy green beans in a can or frozen green beans. You can buy many foods dried, too.

HOW DO YOU CHOOSE FRESH, FROZEN, DRIED, OR CANNED?

❊ Try a food in several forms. Choose the one you like the best. Dried foods can make a great snack!

❊ Many fruits and vegetables are ripe in the summer. They are most delicious and have the most nutrients when they are ripe and just picked.

❊ Canned and frozen fruits and vegetables are packed when they are ripest. They are delicious all year round. They are easy to use in cooking.

FROZEN OR FRESH?

Freezing food preserves its nutrients. Frozen vegetables and fruits are as healthful as fresh. Canned foods are as healthful as other cooked veggies.

15

16

IN SEASON

Many fruits and vegetables are only ripe in one season. Tomatoes, peaches, and many other foods are ripe in the summer. Apples are best in the fall. Oranges are ripest in the winter.

You can buy most fruits and vegetables all year long, though. These foods grow in another part of the world. They are shipped to stores. However, most fruits and vegetables taste best when they travel less. They lose nutrients when they travel and sit on shelves.

HEMISPHERES

Earth has two halves—the northern hemisphere and the southern hemisphere. It is winter in the north when it is summer in the south. That is why strawberries grow in South America when it is winter in the United States.

ADDED SUGAR, ADDED SALT

Packaged foods come in bags, boxes, and cans. They are cooked, canned, frozen, dried, or have ingredients added.

Many packaged foods have fat, sugar, or salt added to them. The most healthful foods have little of these ingredients.

SHOPPING TIP

Look for "low sodium," "reduced sodium," or "no salt added." These words are printed on some canned vegetables, beans, and soups. It means the food has little salt.

19

Nutrition Facts

Serving Size ¾ Cup (30g/1.1 oz.)

Amount Per Serving	Cereal	Cereal with ½ Cup Vitamins A&D Fat Free Milk
Calories	110	150
Calories from Fat	0	0
	% Daily Value**	
Total Fat 0g*	0%	0%
Saturated Fat 0g	0%	0%
Trans Fat 0g		
Polyunsatuated Fat 0g		
Monounsaturated Fat 0g		
Cholesterol 0mg	0%	0%
Sodium 140mg	6%	9%
Potassium 20mg	9%	11%

CEREAL

NEW! NEW!

NEW! NEW!

NEW! NEW!

CEREAL

L CEREAL CEREAL

FOOD LABELS

Every packaged food has a food label. The label is on the back, bottom, or side of the package.

The label lists some of the nutrients that are in the food. It shows how much a grown-up should eat each day. Kids should eat less. They do not need as much of each nutrient.

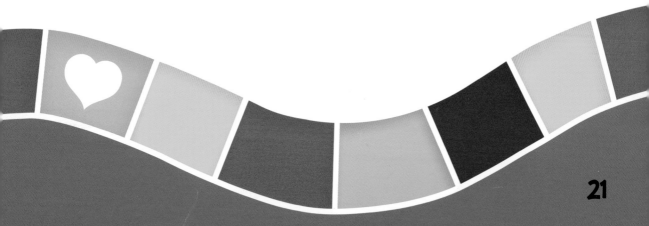

SERVINGS AND CALORIES

The top of the food label says "Serving Size." It also says "Servings Per Container." Many packages have more than one serving. The label says how many servings are in the whole package.

Below, the label tells how many calories are in one serving. A calorie is a unit of measurement. It measures energy. Everyone needs energy. Your body stores extra energy as fat.

Nutrition Facts

Serving Size ¼ Cup (28g)
Servings per Container 12

Amount Per Serving

Calories 110

Calories from Fat 80

23

INGREDIENTS LIST

Below the Nutrition Facts label is a list of ingredients in the food. The list shows ingredients from most to least. There is more of the first ingredient in the food than any other ingredient.

Look for sugar in the ingredients. Foods that list sugar first or second are less healthful. They have more sugar added. Foods with less sugar are more healthful.

OTHER WORDS FOR SUGAR

sugar	rice syrup	fructose
sweetener	maple syrup	dextrose
corn syrup	cane juice	sucrose
high-fructose corn syrup	fruit-juice concentrate	
malt syrup	honey	

THE SUPERMARKET
ISN'T THE ONLY PLACE

Look for farmer's markets and fresh food stands. Fruits and vegetables at these places are usually in season. Some were just picked in the morning!

Visit a farmer's market. Look at all the fruits and vegetables. Ask a grown-up to try something new. Buy some zucchini, kohlrabi, or rutabagas. Try a new recipe!

For the freshest veggies and fruits, grow your own! You can start a garden in a sunny spot. Read a gardening book from the library. Try easy-to-grow veggies first, like lettuce, green beans, and zucchini.

If you don't have a yard, try container gardening. Many vegetables can grow in pots on a windowsill, deck, or patio. Try planting tomatoes, spinach, or beets. Enjoy fresh, healthful food!

GET HEALTHY

1. Choose a food you like. Explore a grocery store to find the different ways it is sold. If you like peaches, find fresh peaches, frozen peaches, canned peaches, and dried peaches. Try each form and keep notes. Which forms do you like the best? Now try this with a food that is less familiar to you.

2. Help your family save money on food. Look at food ads to find foods that are on your shopping list. Clip the coupons. Then find the foods in the store.

3. Ask your teacher or principal to start a garden at your school. Tell them you will learn about plants and nutrition and get exercise at the same time. The best part is taking home your share of the vegetables and fruits!

4. Cooking with your family can be fun. And it makes the most of your helpful planning and shopping. Help your grown-ups choose a new recipe each week, and then be in charge of making the shopping list for its ingredients.

5. Find a fruit or vegetable you have never tried before. Ask your parents if you can buy it and try it out!

WORDS TO KNOW

aisles—walkways between shelves.

calories—a measure of the energy that food gives you.

energy—being able to do things without feeling tired.

fuel—something that is used up to make energy.

grains—starchy seeds from grasses; also called cereals, such as rice, wheat, and barley.

ingredient—one part in a mixture.

nutrients—the parts of food your body needs to live and grow.

packaged—sold in a box, bag, or other container.

preserve—to keep fresh for use later.

protein—a nutrient your body needs to build cells and to grow.

LEARN MORE

BOOKS

Burstein, John, and Goodbody, Slim. *Grocery Shopping: It's in the Bag*. New York: Crabtree, 2008.
Rockwell, Anne. *At the Supermarket*. New York: Henry Holt, 2010.
Weiss, Ellen. *Math at the Store*. New York: Scholastic, 2007.

WEB SITES

To learn more about smart food shopping, visit ABDO Group online at **www.abdopublishing.com**. Web sites about smart food shopping are featured on our Book Links page. These links are routinely monitored and updated to provide the most current information available.

INDEX